© 2020 by Cheryl Hurt, J.D.
All rights reserved. No part of this publication may be reproduced, distributed, or transmitted in any form or by any means, including photocopying, recording, or other electronic or mechanical methods, without the prior written permission of the publisher, except in the case of brief quotations embodied in critical reviews and certain other noncommercial uses permitted by copyright law.

Printed in the United States of America
First Printing, 2020
ISBN:
Partnership for Change
PO Box 1096
Chestertown, MD 21620
www.partnershipforchange.org

Preface:

As a non-profit executive, I have had the pleasure of managing a non-profit organization whose primary source of funding was through the operation of a local thrift store. I have had the experience working through many of these issues on a practical level, both behind the scenes in admin, and on the sales floor.

Running a thrift store is a lot of work but it can also be a whole lot of fun! Thrift stores are both a business and a public service. There's a lot to consider, and some careful planning to undertake, but once you do it will be worth it.

Table of Contents

So you want to open a thrift store? 4
    Nonprofit or For-profit ventures.............5
Regulations...7
    Consignment Sales 8
    Online Sales...9
Inventory Basics 11
    Getting your inventory.............................11
    Inventory management...........................14
        Indirect Inventory Costs: 18
Accounting..22
    Overhead..23
    Banking 26
Marketing..28
Staffing..37
    Volunteers 37
    Interns 38
    Community Service 39
    Paid Staff..40
    Recognition..42
Customer Service 44
    Customer Etiquette 45
    Final Thoughts 49

So you want to open a thrift store?

Thrift stores, Consignment and re-sale shops are all the rage in the current economy, and with good reason. Wages have not kept pace with expenses and many people are struggling to make ends meet. Thrift stores offer the opportunity for people to purchase gently used high quality items at bargain prices and, if run by a nonprofit, help support programs that benefit the community.

Donating and purchasing items at thrift stores and resale shops is recycling at its best. You are keeping items out of landfills that are perfectly usable and helping to extend their useful life in a throw-away society. Your money is also recycled back into the community in the form of programs (if run by a nonprofit) and income, helping to contribute to the economy as a whole.

Nonprofit or For-profit ventures

There was a time that only non profits operated thrift stores. The IRS Code even identifies the operation of a thrift store as a charitable purpose as it serves the needs of the community for low cost items. In recent years many enterprising individuals have opened up for-profit thrift stores, and while this is not the norm, it is done.

The challenges of a for-profit model have to do with both the optics and the operation of the business. For optics, people expect the organization behind a thrift store to be involved in some public good beyond the provision of lower cost items. Thrift stores, in general, have perception problems in that there will always be those who will complain that the prices are too high because the inventory is "free", notwithstanding that the other overhead costs are not free.

The provision of services outside the general operation of the store help with community goodwill that is otherwise not available to for profit businesses. Additionally, the general public often takes issue with just giving people their inventory so they can make a profit. There has to be a trade-off, either in the form of cash or a donation receipt.

As to operational challenges, you will have specific challenges in obtaining inventory and staffing. There may be some who will donate items, but since those donations are not tax-deductible you will find that donors will first send their items to qualified charities. While it is true that most people never hit the threshold to deduct those items, they still are more prone to donate to a charitable organization rather than a for-profit venture. Additionally, it is highly unlikely that you will have any volunteer support, so you will have to rely solely on paid staff.

Location, Location, Location.

Finding the right location is critical for any retail business, but for a thrift store you have to consider both walk up and drive up access. This is important for both donation drop-offs and customer purchases. You also need to consider high visibility. A highly visible location with good signage will provide the bulk of your marketing needs and reduce the need for additional paid advertising.

Regulations

All of the normal business regulations apply to the running of a thrift store. Zoning, Taxes, Payroll, PCI compliance, Licenses and all of the other things that every business needs to manage are as much a part of a thrift store as they are any other business.

If you're a nonprofit, then add the fiduciary responsibilities of nonprofit management on top of that. A thrift store is considered a program, and whether it's a program that funds other programs or is your only program, the same fiduciary rules apply.

For nonprofits, accepting items valued over $250 requires providing a donation receipt to the donor that can be used for tax purposes. Items donated with a value of $500 or more require a Form 8283 to be provided for the donor to fill out. Best practice is to offer donation receipts to all donors. IRS regulations require that the *donor* fill out the value of their donated items.

Donors will often ask that you fill in the value. They may even insist that their accountant, the IRS, or some other authority told them that you should place the value for them, but it is not something that you should do. Even if you will be the one to price the item, it is still up to the donor to fill in that information. If the item comes in with an independent appraisal, then you can use that...but they should attach that appraisal to their receipt.

Consignment Sales

There was a time when consignment sales were considered unrelated business income but that rule has since changed. Consignment sales can now be offered in a thrift store; however, you still have a certain problem with perception. People come into a thrift store expecting bargain-basement pricing and consignment items are necessarily higher priced. This works well if you have a boutique store, and sometimes even a boutique section of your general store. But on the general sales floor, those items are not likely to move.

Online Sales

Whether or not you choose to do any online sales is something you should consider carefully. There are new state and federal reporting requirements and regulations for ecommerce that need to be addressed.

Should you decide to venture into online sales, you will first want to consider what items you intend to showcase in your online boutique. Since these items will likely be sold to customers out of the area, you should consider the shipping costs and how you will manage that part of the sales transaction.

You will also need to manage online items so that they are not sold twice. You can choose to keep those items off of the sales floor, or keep them in a secured display area. Whichever option you choose is fine, so long as you are able to effectively manage your inventory without running the risk of duplicate sales. The negative experience that occurs if you have to cancel an online transaction because the item isn't available will do significant damage to your reputation as a seller, and you should do everything you can to make sure that doesn't happen.

You will also need to determine who will be in charge of online marketing, photography, and sales fulfillment. Often, a dedicated staff member is best as those involved in the day-to-day sales will generally be too busy to give it much attention. Online sales require a specific skill set and understanding the nuances of SEO and social media algorithms to market appropriately.

Inventory Basics

Getting your inventory

Under the nonprofit model

     For the thrift store run by or as a non-profit, you will receive all of your inventory from community donations. The purchase and resale of inventory does not fall under a charitable purpose and those transactions would fall under UBIT (unrelated business income tax) and will be subject to the corporate tax rate. The current threshold for filing the additional forms necessary for reporting UBIT is $1,000, which adds up fast. And that's more paperwork…who wants that!

     Additionally, should your unrelated business income fall above a certain threshold, currently 20%, of your total income, you run the risk of jeopardizing your nonprofit status. The rules on UBIT are complicated and will require an accountant who is well-familiar not only with nonprofit accounting but the special rules regarding unrelated business income.

You are best to stay in the safe harbor of only re-selling donated items. While the inventory is not purchased, there are additional manpower costs that are involved. In fact, these manpower costs apply to both types of stores, and we'll go over that later when we address expenses.

Under the for-profit model

Thrift stores run as a for-profit business are not subject to UBIT as they will file all income under the same corporate (or individual) tax rate. You may see a greater mix of new and used items in these stores as they seek to find the right niche. Donated items are harder to come by for for-profit stores as the donations are not tax deductible.

In our consumer driven society, many people are just looking to get rid of their excess; however, there is a strong motivation to feel that they are doing good with their excess and not just throwing it out.

Some of the places you will be able to find your inventory would be:

- Estate clean outs
- Yard Sale leftovers
- Thrift Store Sales
- Auctions
- Storage Unit Sales
- Wholesale purchases
- Consignment Sales from local vendors

Inventory management

In retail, and thrift stores are subject to much of the same rules as any other retail store, it's all about the sell-through rate. You want items to MOVE, partly because you are relying on the income, and partly because you need to manage the flood of incoming items.

Deciding what you will take

Deciding what you will take has as much to do with your mission as it does with your space. If you have a small, boutique location, you will need to be far more specific about what you will and won't take. Managing space is much more difficult in a smaller location.

If you have a nice large location, you can expand what you take. You may have room for furniture and other large items that a smaller space cannot handle.

Clothes and Books deserve special mention. If you take clothes and books, that may be all you will be able to take! Well, maybe not all, but it will completely consume you. If that is your mission, then be prepared for lots of sorting, laundering, and regular re-organizing.

Electronics are also something you will want to be careful about. People often donate computers with personal information readily accessible, so unless you have a trusted staff member who can effectively clear that data, it's best to refrain from taking those items. On the other hand, they may have completely wiped the hard drive so that it's not of any value to the average consumer. There doesn't seem to be a middle ground on this one so proceed with care. If you can partner with a computer repair professional, that would be helpful.

Older electronics such as analog TVs and large projection TVs will not move and will take up valuable floor space. You will also have to decide whether you will test the items to see if they work, and whether or not you will provide any form of guarantee if they do not work. Will you accept a return? How long after the sale? Will you provide a place for the customer to test the item?

Deciding when certain items will be accepted

Will you have special hours for donations or will you take donations whenever you are open? Will you have a place for drop offs when you are not open? Whichever you decide, you will need to make arrangements for staffing and management of incoming items. It is never recommended to leave the donation processing area unattended, as that will result in a large number of items being left over and above your stated maximums as well as items that you do not take, resulting in additional waste disposal expenses and exhausted staff!

Sales

Regardless of how careful you are with your inventory management, you are quite likely to have far more incoming donations than outgoing sales, so things will start to pile up. Then there's also the issue of seasonal items. How will you manage your excess? Will you have regular price reductions based upon how long the item has been in stock? Will you have scheduled clearance sales? Both are great ways to address aging stock, as long as you have a plan.

Disposing of excess

Sometimes you will get too much. Sometimes you will get broken and unsaleable items. Sometimes you will get items that you don't accept. Sometimes you will get items that you would otherwise accept, but they are out of season. You will need a plan to deal with these items.

If you receive items that are in good condition but that you don't otherwise accept, one great option is to re-donate those items to another local thrift store that does take those items.

Many times you will receive items that just can't be sold. Everything from broken toys & glassware, non-functioning electronics, and other generally ruined items. For those, you will need to make arrangements for regular and bulk item trash removal. This can be a substantial cost.

Indirect Inventory Costs:

Pickup of donated items

If your location is convenient, you will likely receive the bulk of your donations from drop-offs. For this you will need staff to receive the donations and provide donation receipts to donors.

Some donors are not able to get their items to the store, this is often for large estate and moving clean outs. When these requests come in, it is a good idea to visit the location and identify the types of items you are willing to take and then make arrangements for pick up on another day. If you are fortunate enough to have the staffing and time, you can do that on the same day, but often that needs to be scheduled separately.

If your organization has a truck, or access to one, you can schedule those pick ups when you have the staffing to do so. If you do not have access to a truck, or if it is a large number of items then you may wish to rent a larger moving truck.

Storage of donations

Depending on the size of your facility, you may be able to get most of your donations out on the floor, but once you've been open for any length of time you will find that donations exceed your floor space and you may need to find additional space to store out of season items and excess donations. I highly recommend not feeling pressure to provide storage for these extra items, but to manage your donations within your existing space. Unless you have highly valued seasonal items or are operating a small boutique location, storage is an additional expense that is rarely worth the cost.

Sorting and cleaning inventory

Donated items need to be sorted by type and suitability. You will receive plenty of broken items and things that just won't sell. However, all items need to be assessed carefully as you may miss some hidden treasures such as valuable antiques and expensive jewelry.

Most of the items you receive will need some sort of cleaning before placing it out on the sales floor. That can vary from a simple wipe down to more serious scrubbing. You will need to determine if it's worth the additional time.

Pricing inventory

You may have some standard pricing for certain items, but in the beginning you will start doing quite a bit of research to determine appropriate pricing.

Decide in the beginning if your prices are firm or negotiable. Firm pricing with regular markdowns or clearance sales is preferable. If you decide that you are negotiable, you will need to decide who has authority to reduce prices. If the person with pricing authority has other duties (and of course they do!), they will never get anything done because they will be constantly interrupted with requests. People will quickly figure out who that is and will bypass your trusted and well-trained staff members in order to negotiate pricing.

If your pricing is firm, you will still be asked regularly "how firm are your prices?", "can you do better?", "this is scratched/broken/stained/etc, will you take less?" And no, it won't only be on the expensive items, you will get the same questions on items from $0.50 and up! For these reasons, it's important to establish a pricing policy from the beginning.

Accounting

Accounting is both the overall bookkeeping for your company as well as your point of sale accounting practices. The for-profit company will need to track the hard costs of any purchased items in their records whereas the non-profit relies solely on donated items but will need to track donors of both cash and items.

The nonprofit is a fiduciary, so a higher level of responsibility in financial accounting applies, as does donor acknowledgment procedures. Aside from those specific differences, the accounting process is nearly the same. A robust software program will be helpful, but you can go old school with paper records if you prefer, so long as you keep your income and expenses organized into proper categories and balance your accounts regularly.

Overhead

If you are a nonprofit, you may not have the cost of purchased inventory, but that is just a small part of the total overhead costs for running your operation.

Your overhead costs will include the following: Rent, Utilities, Staffing, Marketing and Inventory Expenses. Yes, even donated inventory has associated expenses.

Rent

Expect to pay full market rent regardless of whether or not you are a for-profit or non-profit venture. Landlords rarely are moved by your charitable purpose and your only real negotiating power is whether or not the property has remained vacant in a down economy. There's no real up-side for the landlord to donate the space on a long-term basis. Expect that the longer you are in your location, the longer lease terms your landlord will want.

Utilities

Perhaps you can negotiate that into the rent, but that just means higher rent payments. Your landlord will either be familiar with the costs and adjust the rent accordingly, perhaps even higher to account for the expectation that tenants are generally more mindful of utilities that are under their control rather than those that are perceived as "unlimited."

Phone

A business phone line is a virtual necessity as people will definitely call. They will call for your hours. They will call to ask what donations you accept. They will call to ask about pick ups and/or deliveries. They will even call to see if you have some specified item in stock. They might even call to chat about your organization and what you do for the community. Finally, you will get unnecessary sales calls. Aside from the irritating sales calls, all of the other calls are mostly necessary to the efficient and profitable running of your business.

You may choose a landline phone or a dedicated cell phone, but whichever you choose you will need to make sure it is available during business hours and advertised on your business cards and website and other marketing materials so that you can be contacted.

Internet

Internet service may or may not be critical to your business depending on your specific needs and location. Business internet costs are generally higher than residential rates, so those increased costs are to be expected.

Reasons why you may need internet service:

- If you are using your location for administration or have a need to do internet research or any other connected computer usage at the location.
- Cell phone service is spotty and you want to use WIFI calling.
- Credit card processing using an internet connection will free up your phone line. Some credit card processing equipment has the ability to send the data over either phone lines or internet. If you choose to send the information over phone lines, it will impact your phone use and can also slow down transactions if incoming calls interfere with outgoing transmissions.

Banking

Business Checking Account

You will need a business checking account, which may carry some additional fees and documentation than are required for personal accounts. Business accounts are necessary for merchant credit card processing as well as accepting checks made out to the business, and they're just more professional.

Merchant Credit Card Account

Thrift stores used to only accept cash, and sometimes there is a perception that they still do; however, the reality is that most people expect to be able to use their credit or debit cards, and you will lose sales if you don't accept them.

You can start with accepting only Cash and Checks, but your sales will be stunted until you start accepting credit cards. In order to get the best rates, you will need a bit of history for the store. In the beginning, many businesses start with online providers such as Square & PayPal, but as your business grows you may find that you can negotiate lower rates based on your total sales volume.

Credit card processing companies abound and this will take some research to find the right company with the best rate for your business. Processing fees can vary, and much of it will depend on your sales volume, so it benefits you greatly to keep a close eye on cash vs credit card sales and to contact your processor at least yearly to negotiate rates. There are many competitors in the marketplace now so you may be able to leverage rates that help maximize your bottom line.

Investigate your Merchant Providers because someone will need to be responsible for PCI compliance and network management. Online providers like Square and PayPal handle the PCI compliance but have a higher fee, currently skirting just under 3%. Depending on your volume, the convenience may or may not be worth it.

Marketing

Marketing is not just your typical advertising budget, but we are also talking about product presentation. As you begin to do some market research, you should tour other thrift stores in various locations. You will find a mix of stores that use different marketing schemes.

Many use the typical retail store marketing concept consisting of shelves and sections of related items. This is a functional set up and works fine for some areas, but it doesn't provide a visually appealing shopping experience. You will get those who are looking for specific items, but it doesn't really engage the customer and pull in those impulse sales that you really want.

Some stores, especially boutique stores, employ a more advanced marketing concept where you may find related sections but also larger sections that are staged in living area concepts (think IKEA). These types of stores provide a visually appealing experience for the customer as well as provide an opportunity for them to visualize their purchase in their own home. This requires a more artistic vision but the yield in terms of sales and positive customer feedback and retention are worth the extra work.

Regardless of your large-scale marketing concept, some things are universal. Items must be clean, in good condition, and placed in a visually appealing manner with related items. People like to browse, but they also like to do so in some sort of an organized manner. Providing comfortable seating arrangements are also helpful as it encourages customers to relax and engage with your inventory.

Signage

Your biggest marketing will come from your exterior signage. Nothing beats a great sign for driving in traffic. Your sign should have street appeal and be clearly visible. Banners and flags are also helpful as supplemental signage and can help bring in passers by.

Advertising

A lot of your advertising will be trial and error. Tracking success on your ads is something you should consider. Getting the word out in the beginning is crucial, and if your location is highly visible, you shouldn't need a lot beyond great signage and a good social media campaign.

Print Media

Print media is old school but still functioning. You should track it, but your funding might best be reserved to major sales promotions.

Social Media

Most people are connected these days, and getting a read on what social media outlet connects best with your customer base is important. You shouldn't ignore other forums, but focusing on your primary one will yield the best results. Regular posting of content that engages your customer, but is not "salesy" is important to maintain engagement and increase reach. Sales related posts should be limited to about 10% of your overall postings. It's "Social" Media and no one will be engaged with sales-only posts, they want to get to know the people behind the business.

     As of this writing, Facebook is the primary social media outlet for the thrift store demographic, among those who use social media. It's important, but it shouldn't be your only focus. Instagram and others skew younger, so if you have staff or volunteers that are regularly using those sites, they are worth some attention. Instagram is owned by Facebook and is a very visual medium so having a staff member or volunteer who understands how to capture just the right photo and post to your account is important.

     Unlike with other forms of advertising, Social Media doesn't end with the post, there is account management involved as you will receive comments and questions that need responses. These comments and responses will also help to grow your account and increase your reach.

     Getting reach on social media platforms can be challenging, especially in the beginning, but once you hit certain parameters, the algorithms swing into your favor and you will get some momentum. Currently, 1,000 Facebook "Likes" seems to be the tipping point for increased exposure.

Email lists

People have a love/hate relationship with email lists. It's important to maintain a list and to send out updates, but it should be used in a thoughtful manner. People will want advance notice of sales, closures, and any changes. If you have special events or donor recognition, that is also something you should send out to your regulars.

There are both paid and free bulk email providers, and most will provide you with some analytics to determine your open rate so that you can determine the effectiveness of your email campaign.

You will also need to comply with the CAN-SPAM act, which requires a clear opt-out feature among other requirements. Aside from the penalties for failing to abide by the act, it's really bad public relations and will hurt your business in the long run. Your safe harbor is to have an Opt-In sign up and make sure your unsubscribe link is clear.

Providers such as Constant Contact and Mail Chimp have initiated safeguards to help you stay within the guidelines.

Radio/TV

Radio and TV can be expensive, so do your cost analysis to determine if this is something you feel is helpful to your business.

Brochures

Brochures are important, and if you're a nonprofit that has other programs, they can be helpful. If you're new and are pivoting with changes in services, you should do small print runs. Once you're more established, you can save a bit and do larger print runs.

Website

These days a website is expected, it's basically your online brochure. Securing a domain name and having at least a single information page will help customers find you, and learn more about what you sell and what you take in the way of donations as well as hours and contact information.

A Facebook business page is a great supplement to your website, and it's free. There are constant changes to their algorithm, but it's a valuable social media platform and should be used to maximize your community reach. Not everyone uses social media, so don't rely only on a Facebook business page.

A Google business page is also free and is something that you should have. It's something that shows up in google searches, so it's just one more place to get your name out there. As of this writing, it doesn't require a lot of management, but it does help drive traffic to both your main website and your store.

In fact, you can start with domain forwarding to your Google business page. Purchase the domain name from a registrar and set it up to forward to the URL that Google provides. It's a low-cost way to start your online presence until you grow to something more substantial.

Word of Mouth

This may be "free" but it is customer service and PR driven so your entire operation should be built to provide a positive customer experience from donation to sales.

Product placement

In big box retail stores, there's a marketing schematic to be followed. In smaller boutique stores, it's often up to the creative eye of the owner. In a thrift store, you're pretty much on your own. Depending on the size of the store and the type of merchandise you are carrying, you will need to make sure that the items are well placed, in defined departments, creating a positive customer experience.

Product groupings, as inventory permits, should be placed in areas that suggest their use so that customers can envision them in their home. Not too many so that it looks cluttered, not too few so that it looks sparse.

In-store experience

Providing an environment that brings customers in and one that keeps them browsing is critical to retail success. Product placement that is attractive and functional is critical.

Your in-store displays should be visually appealing. Clean and organized, with like items displayed together. There's both an art and a science to retail displays, and unless your degree is in retail marketing, you may just need to spend some time in market research looking online and by visiting a variety of stores.

Music that appeals to your target audience will keep them browsing and provides an additional stimulus. Music makes a huge difference, and the larger the area the more it helps. Something neutral, perhaps oldies, and of course in-season holiday music will do wonders in keeping your customers in the store browsing and engaging with your inventory and staff.

Business use of music is subject to certain music industry rules and royalty payments (BMI/ASCAP/SESAC). Generally, radio stations are fine and internet radio stations often have low cost plans that include the royalty payments.

Staffing

Finding dedicated and capable staff is a challenge for any business. The for-profit thrift store will need to rely on paid staff. The non-profit variety may be able to benefit from volunteers, interns and community service workers.

Volunteers

Volunteers are great. They are essentially free. They do not cost in terms of dollars, but they will cost you considerably in time. Volunteer staff is not as easy to find as you may think, and even harder to manage. A talented Volunteer Coordinator is worth every penny that you will pay for one, if you are fortunate enough to have the budget to hire them.

In today's economy, volunteers are difficult to find. People are working longer hours and later into life and have far less free time. Even dedicated volunteers will only have precious little time to give to your organization, so you will need to have clearly defined duties and preferably projects that can be broken down into small, manageable *bites.*

Volunteers do not have the financial incentive to show up or risk losing their jobs; their only incentive is the goodwill you develop and their desire to serve the community through your organization. Encouragement, recognition and appreciation are your currency. Be generous with it.

Interns

Interns, if you can get them, can be great but in the nonprofit arena they almost always want to work on policy issues or directly with clients. It is rare to find an intern that wants the retail experience, but there is a chance you could get lucky and find someone from a local college that can get placed with you for work/study hours. You may also cash in on an intern that wants to head up your social media marketing. You will need to reach out to colleges in your area to see what types of students would be available. Know that these are generally short-term placements, generally no longer than a semester.

Community Service

If you are a nonprofit organization, you may be contacted by those who have:
- Court-ordered community service
- Workfare recipients who are referred from the Department of Social Services.
- School-age or College students seeking community service hours.
- Those seeking job training

Some of these "volunteers" will be great and some will require more supervision than you are able to provide. You will be sad when the good ones leave, and do the happy dance when the challenging one's service is completed. If you're really lucky, at least one of them could turn into a great paid employee... but don't hold your breath. The great ones will likely move on to higher paying jobs, but with any luck they'll stay around for a little bit longer.

Paid Staff

Paid staff will be critical for your long-term success. Volunteers will come and go, but if you are trying to build a positive customer experience, you will need stable trained staff. Sadly, this is retail, so you won't be paying top dollar and you likely can't afford to either, so you will get what you pay for. Thrift stores are a unique form of retail and, with the exception of general cashier work, require a particular type of person who can handle donation management. The intake, sorting, cleaning, pricing and marketing of items is a unique skill set and finding individuals who are adept at that is a treasure hunt in and of itself.

Short-term hiring can often be done with contract labor, but long-term and grant funded positions will need to be hired as a standard employee. Either way, you will need to make provisions in your accounting in order to file the appropriate independent contractor and/or employee forms for taxes and reporting.

    Regardless of the type of staffing you have; you will need insurance. You will need Property insurance, liability insurance, unemployment and worker's compensation insurance (once you have paid staff). There are certain protections afforded to organizations and their volunteers, but indemnifying your volunteers and Board members should be a priority.

Recognition

Whether your staff is paid, interns, or volunteers, recognition is a huge part of your staffing considerations. Some volunteers will say they don't want any recognition. Some will mean that, some won't. Some are volunteering to build their resumes, some are doing it because they believe in your vision, and others may have reasons that you can't discern. Regardless of their motivations, recognition is vital as it is their primary payment.

Most nonprofits are cash-strapped and salaries may not be competitive, so recognizing your interns and paid staff is just as important as recognizing your volunteers. You may have separate events for volunteer and staff recognition, and I recommend that you do.

Common ways to recognize volunteers are with special events & outings, awards dinners, certificates and small gifts. Should you have a dinner, it is also a good idea to send a press release and invite the media to the event. For staff recognition, you may want to consider special events, small appreciation gifts, and utilize press releases for promotions, transfers, and retirement.

All of these are great ways to provide special recognition, but never forego the daily positive affirmations and words of encouragement that will keep people coming back. Let them know that you appreciate them every day, not just once a year or at some special event.

Customer Service

Customer Service is critical for every business and a smile and helpful attitude will go far in customer retention and driving sales. Making sure both donors and customers feel valued should be your number one priority. This will not always be easy. You will have some great customers who come in just to see you, and who will buy from you to support your mission. You will also have those who will come in and regularly complain about the prices, always ask for deep discounts, and then still complain when they leave that you basically didn't pay them to take it off your hands!

Then there's the back-end customer service of donors. Many will bring you priceless treasures. Others will bring you their trash. Things they couldn't sell for a quarter at their yard sale but are certain it's worth a fortune. Then there are the stained and broken items that come in with the "someone can use it" statement. No, no they can't. Used or not, no one wants to buy something dirty and broken. Throw it away yourself. Trash removal isn't free to businesses and that eats into your bottom line and ability to provide services. It also takes away from your time in cleaning, sorting, and marketing the products that you can sell.

That said, you will still need to accept every donation with a smile, receiving the priceless with the not-so-priceless with the same amount of grace and appreciation. If it's something that you can't accept, then that requires even more tact when you have to let them know that 'unfortunately, we cannot take these items' or 'regrettably, we are full and can no longer process donations today'.

Customer Etiquette

Some customers are AWESOME! They know what you take and what you don't take. They are considerate of your time and efforts. They check to see what time is good to bring things. They appreciate what you do. They love to support you and think your pricing is on target, or even a little low! We LOVE these customers! They are just amazing and make everything you do worthwhile. They are the reason you do what you do. They make you smile.

Some customers are marginal. They bring you a mix of salable and unusable items. They sneak in items that you don't take. There will be a few broken, dirty, and out of season items but most of it is fine. They sort of care what you take but mostly they just want to get rid of their stuff and expect you'll make an exception or somehow deal with it. They are the bulk of your regular shoppers and can be a mixed bag but you shouldn't have any real problems maintaining a positive experience with them.

Some customers are just UGH! They are demanding. They leave broken, dirty, and unsalable items. They are offended if you don't take their donations for any reason, even if that reason is that you had an emergency closure. If you do deliveries or pickups, they will call 15 times if you don't give them an EXACT appointment time and are 2 minutes late showing up. They complain regularly about your prices saying "you get everything for free" and "this place is always too high". They are the reason you contemplate closing and going to live in a cave somewhere.

Maintaining a pleasant and positive tone with the second two groups can be challenging, but it's critical. After all, we're in business and we need both donors and shoppers to keep going. To be honest, the awesome customers are the minority, but they shine so bright that they keep you going.

Expect to hear a lot of this:
- How clean does it have to be?
    - If you have to ask….
- Can you just take this one item/box/truckload?
    - I know you're closing, but can you please?
    - I know it says you're not taking any more donations, but can you please?
    - I know you don't take these types of things but could you please?
    - I know it's more than you said, but can you make an exception?
- Can you come get this?
- You mean you don't want it?
- It's in pretty good shape
    - Could be anywhere from pristine to falling apart
- I'm sure someone can use it
    - Maybe, but if you wouldn't gladly give it to your child or

best friend, then no, no one wants to pay for something that might work once or twice before breaking down.
- It worked the last time I used it
  - That could be anywhere from this morning to 20 years ago before being stored away somewhere.
- Are your prices firm?
  - Will you take [this much]?
  - Can you do any better on this?
  - Why is this so high?
  - Who does your pricing?

Final Thoughts

Running a thrift store can be exhausting, both mentally and physically. It can also be rewarding and a whole lot of fun! You may become appalled by consumer waste and equally amazed at how people will get rid of perfectly good items knowing that it's because they bought something else new and shiny.

You will be the first to come across unique treasures of unknown value. You'll have the pleasure of seeing how your store serves a community that has a real need for low cost items. And you will go to work every day knowing that you are part of the solution to some of our societies economic and ecological problems.

Welcome to the world of thrifting…you are now a true insider!